Violence in Video Games

by Diane Marczely Gimpel

Content Consultant
Clay Calvert
Professor of Mass Communication
University of Florida

CORE
LIBRARY

Published by ABDO Publishing Company, PO Box 398166, Minneapolis, MN 55439. Copyright © 2013 by Abdo Consulting Group, Inc. International copyrights reserved in all countries. No part of this book may be reproduced in any form without written permission from the publisher. The Core Library™ is a trademark and logo of ABDO Publishing Company.

Printed in the United States of America, North Mankato, Minnesota
112012
012013

Editor: Karen Latchana Kenney
Series Designer: Becky Daum

Cataloging-in-Publication Data
Gimpel, Diane Marczely.
 Violence in video games / Diane Marczely Gimpel.
  p. cm. -- (Hot topics in media)
Includes index.
ISBN 978-1-61783-736-4
1. Violence in video games--Juvenile literature. I. Title.
303.6--dc14
2012946380

Photo Credits: Spencer Platt/Getty Images, cover, 1; Steve Nagy/AP Images, 4; 2K Games/AP Images, 7; Kevin Higley/AP Images, 9; J. Scott Applewhite/AP Images, 10; Red Line Editorial, 12; Boyer/Roger Viollet/Getty Images, 14; Keystone/Getty Images, 17; AP Images, 19; Joe Raedle/Newsmakers/Getty Images, 20; Press Association/AP Images, 24; Paul J. Richards/AFP/Getty Images, 26; Bethesda Softworks/AP Images, 29, 45; Kevork Djansezian/Getty Images, 32; Justin Sullivan/Getty Images, 35; Joe Seer/Shutterstock Images, 37; Francois Guillot/AFP/Getty Images, 38; Jonathan Nackstrand/Getty Images, 40

CONTENTS

CHAPTER ONE

Death and Video Games

Fourteen-year-old Michael Carneal liked to play *Quake, Doom,* and *Redneck Rampage.* These video games have scenes in which the player shoots to kill. In December 1997, Carneal killed three students and hurt five others at Heath High School in Paducah, Kentucky.

Mitchell Johnson played *Mortal Kombat.* In this video game, characters fight to the death. Johnson, 13,

Michael Carneal is brought to the courthouse for a hearing about the Heath High School shootings.

Mortal Kombat

The video game *Mortal Kombat* is bloody. Characters fight each other in the game. The player controls a character's arms and legs so he or she kicks and punches an opponent. If the player wins the battle, his or her character has the option of killing the loser. In some versions, characters can cut a person in half and behead them.

and his 11-year-old cousin Andrew Golden killed five people and hurt ten others outside Westside Middle School in Jonesboro, Arkansas, on March 14, 1998.

On May 20 and 21, 1998, 15-year-old Kipland Kinkel killed his parents in Springfield, Oregon. Then he went to Thurston High School and killed two people and hurt 22 others. Kinkel liked to play *Doom*. This video game involves shooting a gun at monsters and villains.

These boys all played violent video games. They also committed acts of extreme violence. Are the two things connected? Or are they independent of each other?

6

Many video games, such as *Borderlands 2*, involve shooting and destruction.

Gamers and Tragedy

A big issue with some video games is the violence they contain. Concerns often stem from real-life tragedies involving children and teens who played violent video games. These games involve pretend shooting, blood, and gore. Some believe playing violent video games causes players to act in violent ways. Others disagree. Science has not proven that playing violent video games causes violent behavior.

School shootings are tragic and scary. They are also rare. According to the National Center for Education Statistics, 17 kids were killed in US schools during the 2008–2009 school year. More than 55 million children were enrolled in schools that same year.

The public reacts strongly to school shootings because schools should be safe places for children. People want to understand why school shootings happen. They also want to prevent them from happening again. These tragedies are sometimes blamed on violent video games, including the Columbine High School shootings on April 20, 1999. At the time, it was the deadliest school shooting in US history.

Tying Tragedy to Technology

The day of the Columbine shootings, the *Rocky Mountain News* published an online story asking who was to blame. One possibility listed was violent video games because the killers liked to play them.

Students were evacuated from the school after the deadly Columbine shootings occurred.

President Bill Clinton talks with students at T.C. Williams High School in Alexandria, Virginia, about school violence in 1999.

Other newspapers also noted the killers' interest in violent video games. Some experts suggested a link between video game violence and real-life violence because some players of violent video games behaved violently.

In his weekly radio address just after the Columbine shootings, US president Bill Clinton spoke about media and violence. He mentioned David

Grossman, a psychologist and former military officer who said video games teach children to kill like military training programs do. But video games do not provide the character training that people in the military get. Clinton asked parents not to buy their children violent video games. He also asked media and entertainment companies to put less violence in movies, television shows, and video games.

The Debate

Video games first came into public use approximately 25 years before the Columbine massacre. They have since exploded in popularity. In 2011 video game sales reached between $16.3 and $16.6 billion.

Who Plays Video Games?

- The average video game player is 30 years old and has been playing video games for 12 years.
- Sixty-eight percent of video game players are 18 or older.
- Parents are present 90 percent of the time when games are bought or rented.

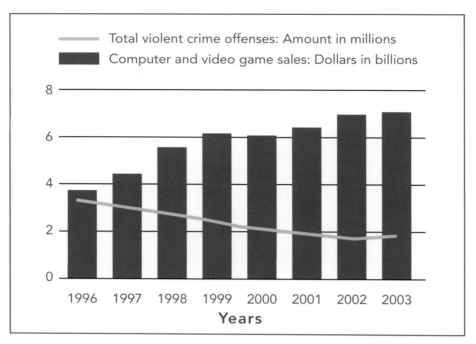

Violent Crime and Video Game Sales

The chart above shows the number of violent crimes in the United States and the amount of video game sales from 1996 to 2003. What does this graph tell you about violence in video games and violent crime? Does it support one side of the debate? Which one?

Approximately 99 percent of boys and 94 percent of girls play video games.

These statistics worry some people. They believe playing violent video games causes some people to be less kind toward others, or to even hurt or kill. But violent crime statistics should go up if that were true. While the number of people who play violent video games has increased, the violent crime rate has gone down. In fact some believe violent video games help players cope with mean thoughts and anger without hurting anyone. The debate continues on violent video games and their effects. Video games have not always contained violent action. They started simply and evolved rapidly over the decades.

CHAPTER TWO

Video Games Evolve

Debate about violent video games did not begin with school shootings in the 1990s. And it did not end there. The debate started soon after violent video games first became available.

After the end of World War II (1939–1945), companies turned military technology into simple games. The first was a missile game designed in 1947. The device's creators were Thomas T. Goldsmith Jr.

The first video game was based on World War II radar displays.

The Nimrod Computer

The first computer designed to play a game was the Nimrod computer. It was made in England in May 1951. The computer played a game called *Nim*. Players of the game took turns removing tokens from piles. The game ended when the last token was taken.

and Estle Ray Mann. They were physicists who based the game on World War II radar displays. Players used knobs to adjust the angle of light beams. These beams represented missiles aimed at targets. The game, however, was never sold to the public.

The First Video and Computer Games

One of the first video games was *OXO*. Players used it to play tic-tac-toe. The game was created at Cambridge University in England in 1952. It was not available to the public. *Tennis for Two* was another early video game. US physicist William A. Higinbotham developed the game in 1958 at Brookhaven National Laboratory in Upton, New York.

A boy plays the game *Noughts and Crosses* on his television in 1975.

It was like table tennis. The public was allowed to play *Tennis for Two* at the lab. Hundreds waited in line for hours to play the game.

One of the first computer games that allowed players to control the action was *Spacewar!* In *Spacewar!* players controlled a spacecraft that fired missiles. It was developed at the Massachusetts Institute of Technology in 1961. The game was later installed on a new computer. It could also be passed from one computer to another.

In 1967 engineer Ralph Baer and his fellow workers created two games that could be played on a television. On May 24, 1972, the games were released on the Magnavox Odyssey, the first home video game system. One hundred thousand Odysseys sold in six months. A year before that, in 1971, the first mass-produced video arcade game was released. It was called *Computer Space*. Nolan Bushnell and Ted Dabney were its creators. They founded the Atari video game company in 1972. Their first game that sold well was *Pong*. It was an electronic ping-pong game released in 1975.

Later in the 1970s and early 1980s came other wildly popular video games: *Space Invaders, Asteroids, Pac Man,* and *Donkey Kong.* As time went on, more companies developed and sold video games and video game consoles. New games had better and more realistic graphics and sound. They also were

Atari developed home gaming systems used with televisions.

more difficult to play. Over the years, many billions of video games have sold worldwide.

Violence in Video Games

The first debate over video game violence involved the game *Death Race*, released in 1976. In this game, stick-figure cars ran over stick-figure gremlins. Author

A player shoots a fake gun to play an arcade video game.

Steven L. Kent wrote that the game upset people because the gremlins cried when hit, and then a gravestone would pop up.

By 1992 video game graphics had moved beyond stick figures to more realistic images. *Mortal Kombat* was released that year. It showed blood and gore as characters fought and killed each other. That game and another called *Night Trap* sparked concern over how children would be affected by watching such violent images. These concerns led US senators

Joseph Lieberman and Herbert Kohl to ask Congress to pass a law banning violent video games. But Congress did not vote on the law. Instead stores voluntarily stopped selling *Night Trap*. Then in 1994 the video game industry formed the Entertainment Software Rating Board (ESRB). The ESRB puts ratings on video games based upon the amount of violence, bad language, and adult content in them. The ESRB assigns age and content ratings for video games. The ratings warn parents of the content in the games.

Doom was another game that led to the creation of the ESRB. *Doom* was among the first games to have a first-person shooter perspective. This means

Doom levels

The object of *Doom* is for the player to escape a multi-level environment while shooting at monsters and bad guys. A level is an area or scene within a game. In *Doom* the action takes place on Mars, its moons, and the underworld. The player's goal is to get past demons and other threats to find the exit and get to the next level.

Rating	Age	Description	Examples
EC: Early Childhood	3+	Nothing inappropriate	*Dora the Explorer, Animal Adventures*
E: Everyone	6+	Minimal cartoon, fantasy, mild violence and/or infrequent use of mild language	*Lego Star Wars, NFL Head Coach*
E10+: Everyone 10+	10+	More cartoon, fantasy, and mild violence, mild language and/or minimal suggestive themes	*Shadow the Hedgehog, Harry Potter and the Goblet of Fire*
T: Teen	13+	Violence, suggestive themes, crude humor, minimal blood, simulated gambling and/or infrequent use of strong language	*Super Smash Bros. Melee, Tomb Raider: Legend*
M: Mature	17+	Intense violence, blood, and gore, sexual content and/or strong language	*Mortal Kombat Deception, Halo 2*
AO: Adults Only	18+	Prolonged scenes of intense violence, graphic sexual content and/or nudity	*Manhunt 2*

Video Game Ratings

This chart shows the ratings given to video games by the ESRB. What do the video game ratings tell you about their content? How is this information similar to the chapter's description of the ESRB ratings? How is it different?

that players played from the viewpoint of a person shooting at other characters. *Grand Theft Auto: San Andreas* was another violent game. The ESRB changed the game's rating to "Adults Only" from "Mature." This led stores to stop selling it.

EXPLORE ONLINE

The focus in Chapter Two was the history of video game development. The Web site below describes the history of video games. As you know, every source is different. How is the information given in the Web site different from the information in this chapter? What information is the same? How do the two sources present information differently? What can you learn from this Web site?

Make Kids Count: Video Game History
www.makekidscount.com/?p=3580

CHAPTER THREE

Do Video Games Cause Violence?

There are many concerns about violent video games. Some people think game players might become more violent. Violent games may teach players how to be violent and that violence is acceptable. Others think playing violent games can cause violent thoughts. Or it may make players less upset by real violence.

In the *Call of Duty: Modern Warfare 2* video game, a player has the viewpoint of a person shooting a machine gun.

President Bill Clinton held up an advertisement for a video game about a school bus driving through a war zone in 1999.

Politicians Worry

Politicians have expressed these worries, especially after shootings involving children. In 1999 President Bill Clinton suggested children become numb to the results of violence after seeing violence. In 2001 US attorney general John Ashcroft said violent video games lead young people to behave violently.

And in 2007 US senator Joseph Lieberman said many studies showed children were more aggressive after playing violent video games.

Doctors and Medical Professionals

Some doctors and medical professionals also share these worries. Psychology professor and former military officer David Grossman suggested school shooter Michael Carneal was able to shoot so many people because he trained on video games. In 2000 six US medical groups said violent video games may teach children that violence is a good way to settle conflicts. The groups also said such games may make children behave violently and become less interested in helping victims of violence.

In August 2005, the American Psychological Association asked that violence be reduced in video games played by children and teens. The group also asked game makers to show in their games that violence was bad for everyone.

The Scientific Studies

Different scientific studies support some of these ideas. These studies include six done since 2000. A 2005 study found viewing violent video games made players more aggressive. Another group of scientists found that playing violent video games put players at risk for being physically aggressive. A 2009 study had similar findings.

A second 2009 study showed that college students who played a violent video game had more aggressive thoughts and behavior than those who played a non-violent game.

These studies and opinions suggest that violent video games are not harmless

A Recent Shooting

While scientists continue to study and debate whether video games cause violence, events still happen in which a link is made between the two. In March 2012, Mohammed Merah killed three soldiers and four civilians at a Jewish school in France. The killer's former wife said the two of them used to play *Call of Duty*, a video game in which troops fight to the death.

Each year video game graphics become more realistic and vivid, such as in the game *Dishonored.*

How the Studies Were Done

In some studies, scientists asked people about their favorite video games, how often they played, and their behavior. These studies rely on game players being truthful and having good memories. In other cases scientists had their subjects play video games and gave them behavior tests afterward. These studies rely on the ability of tests to predict how a person would act in the real world.

entertainment. Instead the studies support the theory that violent video games influence thoughts and behaviors in bad ways. These studies and opinions are at odds with others who say this has not yet been proven.

President Bill Clinton gave a radio address about violence in media on April 24, 1998. He said:

> *Parents come first. They should turn off the television, pay attention to what's on the computer screen, refuse to buy products that glorify violence. Make sure your children know you care about what they're doing.*
>
> *And to the media and entertainment industries, I say just this: You know you have enormous power to educate and entertain our children. Yes, there should be a label on the outside of every video, but what counts is what's on the inside and what it will do to the insides of our young people. I ask you to make every video game and movie as if your own children were watching it.*

Source: William J. Clinton. "The President's Radio Address: April 24, 1998." The American Presidency Project. Web. Accessed June 27, 2012.

Consider Your Audience

Read Clinton's speech closely. How could you adapt the speech for a different audience, such as your parents or younger friends? Write a blog post conveying this same information for the new audience. What is the best way to get your point across to this audience?

CHAPTER FOUR

An Ongoing Debate

Some experts say video games do not result in violent behavior. Although some violent people may play violent video games, it does not mean playing violent video games makes people violent.

The Video Game Industry

The Entertainment Software Association (ESA) is a group whose members include video game publishers, such as Nintendo and Ubisoft. The group

People play the newest video games at video game conventions.

says violent crime has decreased since the early 1990s, while video game use has increased greatly.

The ESA also mentions experts who have declared no link exists between violent video games and violence on its Web site.

A Task Force Opinion

Pennsylvania's Task Force on Violent Interactive Video Games said scientific studies had shown a connection between violent video game play and aggression. But this is not the same thing as a cause-and-effect relationship. The 2008 report said violent video games may be a minor factor in

Ratings on covers help parents choose which video games they want their children to play.

making children aggressive. The report also said no solid evidence linked violent video games with real-life violence.

The task force recommended against laws to restrict violent video games. The group noted such laws had been struck down previously by the federal courts because judges said those laws restricted the right to free speech and expression. The task force recommended the creation of education programs for people who buy video games.

The nation's highest court also had its say regarding laws restricting sales of violent video games. On June 27, 2011, the US Supreme Court

The First Amendment

In addition to freedom of expression, the First Amendment of the US Constitution protects religious freedom, freedom of the press, and the right to gather peacefully and ask the government to fix what it has done wrong. Video games qualify for First Amendment protection because they express ideas and tell stories, just like books and television shows.

California governor Arnold Schwarzenegger fought for his state's video game bill, which was later struck down by the Supreme Court.

ruled a California law banning the sale of violent video games to people younger than 18 violated free speech rights. Various courts have also struck down lawsuits filed on behalf of shooting victims against the video game industry.

Video games continue to be popular with kids and adults.

What Scientists Say

Some scientific studies support the idea that video games do not lead to violence. A 2008 study found that college students who played a violent video game were no more aggressive after they finished playing than those who played a nonviolent game. The study stated that players who reported playing a lot of violent video games over a long time behaved no more aggressively than others in the experiment. The study results stated that no one could predict whether a person would become a violent criminal by looking at how much that person played violent video games.

In another study, researchers expected players who played a violent Internet game for a month would become more aggressive, but they did not. Other researchers said violent video games allowed players to experiment with aggression in a safe setting without real-world results.

The Debate Continues

Some say the debate should change. Instead of looking for a cause-and-effect relationship between video game violence and violent behavior, people should look for ways to figure out which children are likely to be influenced by video game violence. People also might focus on other issues that might lead to violent behavior, such as child abuse, access

There are many types of video games to choose from, including the nonviolent game Just Dance 4.

to weapons, and mental health problems. In addition young people can be taught to make decisions about entertainment by thinking about the messages their video games deliver.

The debate continues about the effect violent video games have on the human mind. Video games have been around for only 65 years. More time is likely needed to figure out if they have any effects.

This is an excerpt from a study on the link between video game violence and real violence. The authors wrote:

> The two studies . . . examined the link between violent-video-game playing and violent or aggressive acts in both the laboratory and in real life. No link . . . was found between violent-video-game playing and aggressive or violent acts. Males were generally more aggressive than were females. Some aggressive individuals appeared to self-direct toward choosing violent video games . . . In this article, it is argued that the pathway to violent criminal acts occurs through a combination of . . . genetics or brain injury . . . and exposure to violence in the family. Media violence, particularly video game violence, may have limited or no . . . role.

Source: Christopher J., Ferguson, Stephanie M. Rueda, Amanda M. Cruz, Diana E. Ferguson, Stacey Fritz, and Shawn M. Smith. "Violent Video Games and Aggression: Causal Relationship or Byproduct of Family Violence and Intrinsic Violence Motivation?" Criminal Justice and Behavior 35.3 (March 2008): 330.

What's the Big Idea?

Take a close look at the authors' words. What is the main idea? What evidence is used to support the point? Come up with a few sentences showing how the authors use two or three pieces of evidence to support the main point.

IMPORTANT DATES

1947

Thomas T. Goldsmith Jr. and Estle Ray Mann design a missile game.

1967

The first video games that can be played on a television are developed.

1972

The first home video game system is released.

1994

The video game industry creates the Entertainment Software Ratings Board to rate game content.

1997

Michael Carneal kills three students and wounds five other people at his Kentucky school on December 1.

1998

Mortal Kombat player Mitchell Johnson and his cousin kill five people and wound ten others outside their Arkansas school on March 14.

1975

Pong is released by Atari.

1976

Death Race, a violent video game, is released.

1992

Mortal Kombat is released.

1998

Doom player Kipland Kinkel kills his parents and then goes to his Oregon high school, where he kills two people and hurts 22 others on May 20–21.

1999

The Columbine High School shootings happen on April 20.

2011

The US Supreme Court strikes down a California law restricting the rental or sale of violent video games to minors on June 27.

STOP AND THINK

Say What?

Studying video game violence can mean learning a lot of new words. Find three words in this book you have never seen or heard before. Use a dictionary to find out what they mean. Then write the meanings in your own words, and use each word in a new sentence.

Another View

There are many sources online and in your library about violent video games. Ask a librarian or other adult to help you find a reliable source on violent video games. Compare what you learn in this new source and what you have found out in this book. Then write a short essay comparing and contrasting the new source's view of violent video games to the ideas in this book. How are they different? How are they similar? Why do you think they are different or similar?

Why Do I Care?

This book explains how violence is used in video games. List two or three examples of violence you've seen in video games. Did it look real? How did you feel after you saw the violence?

Surprise Me

The history and debate on violence in video games can be interesting and surprising. What two or three facts about video game violence and the debate around it did you find most surprising? Write a few sentences about each fact. Why did you find them surprising?

GLOSSARY

aggressive
ready or likely to attack
or fight

politician
a person who is involved
with politics

graphics
illustration of characters and
scenes in a video game

psychological
involving the mind; relating
to the emotions and behavior
of a person

massacre
the killing of many people

physicist
an expert in the scientific
study of matter and energy

rampage
a period of violent and
uncontrolled behavior

LEARN MORE

Books

Allman, Toney. *Media Violence*. Yankton, SD: Erickson Press, 2007.

Grayson, Robert. *Sony: The Company and Its Founders*. Minneapolis, MN: ABDO, 2013.

Hermansson, Casie. *Parental Guidance Ratings*. Minneapolis, MN: ABDO, 2013.

Web Links

To learn more about video game violence, visit ABDO Publishing Company online at **www.abdopublishing.com**. Web sites about video game violence are featured on our Book Links page. These links are routinely monitored and updated to provide the most current information available. Visit **www.mycorelibrary.com** for free additional tools for teachers and students.

INDEX

ABOUT THE AUTHOR

Diane Marczely Gimpel is a freelance writer and English teacher. She also is a former newspaper reporter. She lives in the suburbs of Philadelphia, Pennsylvania, with her husband and two sons. This is her sixth book for young readers.